ANIMAL FAMILIES

Wolves

GROLIER
EDUCATIONAL

About this book

Why do many animals gather in family and larger groups? Why do bees dance and wolves howl? How do lions hunt together and zebras defend against them? These and hundreds of other fascinating animal behavior questions are answered in this new set of books about animal life. The books provide fascinating insights into the activities and bodies of all sorts of animals, from meerkat troop signals to honeybee nectar searches, and from ostrich feet to elephant trunks. In each book there are detailed examples of how animals behave, and how they relate to each other. Each book also has lots of photos and specially drawn illustrations. After you have read the book, if you are interested in finding out more about a particular animal, look at the Further Reading section on page 30. It has books and websites to check out. A Glossary on page 31 explains words that you may not be familiar with, and the Index on page 32 tells you where in the book to find a particular animal, behavior, or place.

Published 2001 by Grolier Educational
Sherman Turnpike
Danbury, Connecticut 06816

© 2001 Brown Partworks Limited.

Library of Congress Cataloging-in-Publication Data
Animal Families
p.cm.
Contents: v. 1. Ants/John Woodward — v. 2. Bats/John Jackson — v. 3. Bison/John Woodward — v. 4. Chimpanzees/John Woodward — v. 5. Dolphins/Bridget Giles — v. 6. Elephants/Daniel Gilpin — v. 7. Honeybees/John Woodward — v. 8. Kangaroos/Jen Green — v. 9. Lions/John Woodward — v. 10. Meerkats/Tom Jackson — v. 11. Ostriches/Jen Green — v. 12. Penguins/Daniel Gilpin — v. 13. Prairie Dogs/Jen Green — v. 14. Weaverbirds/Tim Harris — v. 15. Wolves/Jen Green — v. 16. Zebras/Bridget Giles.
ISBN 0-7172-9585-0 (set: alk. paper)
ISBN 0-7172-5500-X (v. 15: alk. paper)
1. Animal behavior—Juvenile literature. [1. Animals—Habits and behavior.]
I. Grolier Educational Corporation.
QL751.5.A565 2001
591.5-dc21
00-042669

Printed and bound in Singapore.

FOR BROWN PARTWORKS LIMITED
Author: Jen Green
Consultant: Dr. Adrian Seymour
Project editor: Tim Harris
Managing editor: Anne O'Daly
Picture research: Adrian Bentley
Index: Margaret Mitchell

PICTURE CREDITS
Artworks: AntBits Illustration

Bruce Coleman Collection: (Erwin & Peggy Bauer) 5 below; (Hans Reinhard) 21 above, 21 below; (Jeff Foott) 9 above, 26; (Joe McDonald) 10; (John Shaw) 5 above; (Rod Williams) 18; (Staffan Widstrand) 24–25. *Corbis*: (Tom Brakefield) 10–11. *Image Bank*: (Joseph van Os) 20. *NHPA*: (Andy Rouse) 6, 13 above; (B. & C. Alexander) 28; (Darek Karp) 29 below; (David Middleton) front cover, 14; (John Shaw) 7 below; (Martin Harvey) 23 above; (Rich Kirchner) 13 below, 19; (T. Kitchin & V. Hurst) 12, 15, 24. *Papilio Photographic*: (Bryan Knox) 16, 17, 27 above. *Still Pictures*: (Carl R. Sams II) 14–15; (Klein/Hubert) title page, 4, 7 above, 8, 9 below; (M. & C. Denis-Huot) 23 below; (Michel Gunther) 22; (Peter Weimann) contents page, 27 below. *Travel Ink*: (Mark Reeve) 29 above.

Series created by Brown Partworks Limited.
Designed by Wilson Design Associates

Contents

Introduction

Wolves are fierce and beautiful creatures. With their strong jaws and sharp teeth they are deadly hunters, but wolves can be gentle and playful, too.

◄ *Wolves and domestic dogs are related and look very alike, too.*

Wolves are creatures of the north. Once they were found throughout the northern hemisphere, but people have hunted them for centuries, and now they are much rarer. Wolves from different parts of the world may look a little different from one another, but they are all one species (type), *Canis lupus*—the gray wolf.

Wolves are canids—members of the dog family. Jackals, coyotes, and foxes are in the same family. So are the domestic dogs we keep as pets because all breeds of tame dogs are descended from wolves.

Most wolves live together in a group called a pack. The main purpose of the pack is for hunting. A group of wolves hunting together can kill prey animals much larger than any individual group member. Elk

and reindeer may fall victims to a wolf pack, but a wolf on its own must be content with hunting smaller prey. Wolf cubs also stand a better chance of surviving if they are born in a pack because all the members of the pack help rear them. Wolves are powerful predators (hunters), with strong legs built for running. They have long snouts and pricked-up ears. Their well-muscled bodies are covered with thick, shaggy fur.

In this book you will find out more about these magnificient creatures, including how they live together in groups, how they find their food, how they care for their young, and how they have been treated by people.

The red wolf

Red wolves are found in the southeastern United States. Smaller than gray wolves, they get their name from their reddish fur. Red wolves were once quite common, but now there are very few left. They were once thought to be a separate species of wolf, but research suggests they are crossbreeds between coyotes and gray wolves.

▲ **Wolves are quite at home in the harshest winter conditions.**

▼ **The red wolf is now endangered.**

The wolf pack

Most packs contain between five and eight wolves. Small packs may have just two members; a large pack may hold 30 wolves.

Each wolf pack is led by the strongest, most experienced male and female. These are called the alpha male and female, after the first letter of the Greek alphabet. The alpha male and female are the only wolves in the pack that produce young. The other group members are usually their children—young cubs and older offspring born in previous years.

All wolf packs are organized according to a strict hierarchy (ranking order). Below the alpha pair are the next most senior wolves, called the beta male and female. Below them come the younger and less experienced wolves. From the top wolves of the pack to the most junior, each animal knows its rank.

Not all wolves live in a pack. Single wolves may be young

► *A solitary wolf will find it more difficult to hunt and kill large prey.*

▼ *Each wolf knows its rank: The three closest wolves are submitting to an alpha male.*

individuals that have left the pack they grew up in and are searching for other wolves to form a new pack. Other lone wolves are old or sickly animals that have been turned out of their group.

Many different kinds of animals have a territory—a patch of land they use for finding food or rearing young, and which they defend against others of their kind. Wolves are no exception. They use their territories for hunting and breeding. The cubs are born in a safe den in the heart of the "patch." A small wolf territory may be only around 36 square miles (100 sq km). Others are huge, covering 360 square miles (1,000 sq km) or more.

▶ *A small wolf pack may contain just three animals, though others can be 10 times this size.*

Marking territory

Groups of wolves defend their territories against rival wolf packs. They mark the borders of their "patch" by spraying smelly urine on logs, rocks, and bushes. Other wolves that pass that way smell the scent and know to keep out of the territory. Each wolf has its own distinctive scent, so pack members can identify one another by these marks.

Communication

Wolves have many different ways of communicating with one another. They can produce a wide range of noises, including snarls, whines, whimpers, squeaks, and barks. Wolves in a pack are mostly friendly and affectionate with one another. When two pack members meet, they whine, wag their tails, and lick one another's fur.

Howling

A wolf's howl is an eerie sound familiar from horror movies! A wolf sticks its nose in the air to produce this drawn-out wail. The other wolves join in with different notes. Wolves howl to contact members of their group that have got separated. Their calls carry over a long distance. They also howl to rally the group before hunting and to warn rival wolf packs to keep away. On hearing the challenge, the other pack may howl back.

▶ *A wolf howl can be heard 6 miles (10km) away.*

Scientists who study wolves have learned that they have many different facial expressions. They also hold their bodies in different ways to show their feelings and express their rank in the pack. Senior wolves hold their head and tail high and stand up straight to look as big as they can. They hold their ears pricked forward, growl, and bare their teeth.

Junior wolves use very different "body language" and expressions. They cower with their head held low to make themselves look small. They lay back their ears,

▲ *The wolf on the left is warning off other pack members.*

▼ *These wolves are good friends!*

whine, and hide their teeth in a tight-lipped grin.

Sometimes a junior wolf will try to climb up the ranking order by challenging an older wolf with a snarl. If the senior wolf snarls back, the young wolf often backs down by rolling on its back and whimpering. Such gestures help soothe ruffled feelings and mean that actual fights are rare.

Tail positions

Wolves use their bushy tails to express their feelings. Normally, the tail droops down, but top wolves raise theirs high in the air. An aggressive wolf lifts its tail bolt upright or curves it outward in a gesture that means "watch out!" Young wolves submit (give way) to their seniors by tucking their tails between their legs.

Finding food

Wolves are carnivores—they mainly eat meat. They prefer to hunt and eat large animals such as moose, muskoxen, elk, and caribou (reindeer). These creatures are powerful and armed with sharp hooves and fierce horns or antlers. They can only be hunted by wolves in a pack.

◄ *These wolves are eating an elk they have killed. A wolf eats up to 11–22 pounds (5–10kg) of meat a day.*

▼ *A chase in the snow: If the hare is healthy, victory is not guaranteed for the wolf.*

Wolves also hunt all sorts of smaller creatures. Beavers, hares, squirrels, mice, birds, even fish and frogs are all on the menu. Wolves also steal domestic animals and eat carrion (dead animals). A hungry wolf will eat fruit and plants or steal into city suburbs to scavenge garbage.

Wolves can see well, but mainly hunt by smell and hearing. Their sensitive nose can catch a faint trace of scent on the wind. Their ears are alert to tiny sounds such as breaking twigs that give away hidden prey.

A hunting wolf pack gradually slinks closer to a herd of grazing muskoxen, moose, or caribou.

The wolves approach upwind so their prey do not sense them. They study the herd and single out young, weak, or injured animals that make easy targets.

When the wolves are spotted, the chase is on! The speediest wolves run on ahead to surround their prey. Then they dart forward to separate young or sick animals. The wolves close in from all sides and attack the creature's rump, neck, and snout.

Finally, a strong wolf leaps up and kills the chosen victim by biting its neck.

A hungry wolf can eat as much as 20 pounds (9kg) of meat in one "sitting." Some meat may be buried for later. If there are young cubs in the den, the wolves hurry back and feed them half-digested meat.

▲ *Closing in for the kill: A small pack of wolves gets ready to surround and kill an elk with an injured leg.*

Lone wolves

Without a pack to hunt with, lone wolves target smaller prey. Nose to the ground, they follow the scent of game birds, hares, squirrels, and mice. When the wolf is close enough, it pounces, catching its victim in its front paws.

Having cubs

Like most members of the dog family, wolves breed only once a year. Mating takes place in late winter. The young develop inside the mother for 63 days before being born.

▼ *A pregnant female wolf often takes over the abandoned lair of another animal to prepare it for the birth of her cubs.*

Wolves time their mating so that the young will be born in spring as the weather gets warmer. However, spring comes later in the north than in the south. In mild southern regions wolves mate in February so that the cubs will be born in April or May. In the icy north they mate about a month later, and there the cubs are born as spring arrives in late May or June.

About six weeks after mating the pregnant female prepares a den for her cubs. She may take over an old fox's lair or porcupine burrow and make it bigger, or nest in a cave or a clump of long grass. When the cubs are due, the other wolves gather outside and howl with excitement. They sniff the air to find out when the babies are born.

Female wolves usually give birth to a litter (group) of five or six cubs. There may be as many as 10 pups in a big litter. Newborn young weigh only

▲ *This female wolf is ready to mate–despite the snowy weather.*

Breeding time

The breeding season is a time of tension in the wolf pack because all the adult animals are ready to breed. The alpha male and female bully the others to prevent them from mating. The alpha female may temporarily force her rivals out of the pack. Once the top wolves have mated, they stop being aggressive. Life in the pack returns to normal again.

1 pound (450g) and are blind, deaf, and helpless. At first, the babies cannot even stand, but the mother pushes them to her nipples, and they begin to suck her milk. Slowly, they gain the strength to lead active lives.

▼ *Newborn cubs will open their eyes first aged two or three weeks.*

Growing up

After only two or three weeks the cubs are bigger and stronger. They can now hear, and their eyes are open so they can see. They clamber over one another to reach the warmest places under their mother's body. By the age of three weeks they are able to stand and wobble to the den entrance to sniff the air and look at the outside world.

▲ *Feeding time often provides an opportunity for some play with brothers and sisters—and mom!*

For the first week or so the cubs feed only on their mother's milk, and she rarely leaves them. The other wolves bring half-chewed meat for her to eat, and soon the cubs begin to eat it too. At the age of three or four weeks it is time to leave the safety of the den for the outside world. As the cubs emerge, the other wolves gather around and wag their tails vigorously. They sniff and greet the new members of their pack.

Now, when an adult wolf returns from hunting, the cubs are ready. They gather around and lick at its mouth begging for food. In response the adult wolf arches its body and regurgitates (coughs up) a warm meal of half-digested meat.

At about eight weeks the cubs no longer depend on their mother's milk. Also around this age they become too big for the den, and they venture out for the first time. Then the pups and the parents move to a safe, open area known as a "rendezvous site." The pups are left there while the other wolves go hunting. One adult wolf usually stays to "babysit" the pups.

Helping out

All the wolves in the pack help bring up the cubs. The father and other adults, who may be the youngsters' grown-up brothers and sisters, help by bringing food and guarding the pups. At about 10 months the young start to help on hunting trips.

▲ *Wolf moms are gentle and protective parents.*

▼ *This three-week-old pup is having a drink of its mother's milk.*

The young begin to learn hunting skills by pouncing on objects that take their fancy, such as flowers or feathers. Soon they start catching live prey such as insects and mice.

The cubs also spend a lot of time play-fighting. It helps them develop the skills they will need for adult life. Gradually, the strongest youngsters begin to dominate the others. By the age of 12 weeks the cubs have developed a "pecking order" that mirrors the hierarchy among the adults of their pack.

Young males

**The cubs spend the summer in a safe, grassy spot near their old den.
By fall they are strong enough to travel with the adults as they roam through
their territory in search of food.**

At the age of 10 months the young wolves are allowed on hunting expeditions. At first, they simply watch what the adults do and learn to keep quiet when the pack is stalking. Later, they act as runners but are not yet old enough to help kill animals.

At one year old the youngsters look like small adult wolves. They reach their full size at the age of 18 months. Most young wolves stay with the pack for two to

▲ A lone male is always careful where it wanders. If caught in the territory of a pack, it may be chased and killed.

▲ *These young wolves have grown enough to join in many of their pack's activities. They may even take part in a hunt.*

three years at least. As they grow older, they learn about hunting.

By the time they are three years old, young males have reached the age when they can breed. Some stay with the same pack all their lives, but many leave at this time. If a young male challenges the leader of his pack and loses, he may be turned out of the group. He will wander far and wide, either on his own or with his brothers. Eventually, if he survives, he may find a single female or a group of sisters and start a new pack.

On the run

The life of a lone male wolf is full of danger. Without a group to hunt with, the young wolf often goes hungry and wanders a long way each day in search of food. Lone wolves are wary and cautious. Wherever possible, they stay out of other wolves' territories. If they are caught trespassing, they may be attacked and killed. In lonely spots away from pack territories the young male howls to find out if a female is near. If she hears his call, a lone female will howl back, and the pair will find each other by their cries.

She-wolves

Young she-wolves reach maturity—the age at which they can breed—even earlier than their brothers. By the time she is two, the young female is able to mate. Now the young she-wolf becomes a threat to her mother. During the mating season alpha females force many of their older daughters out of the pack.

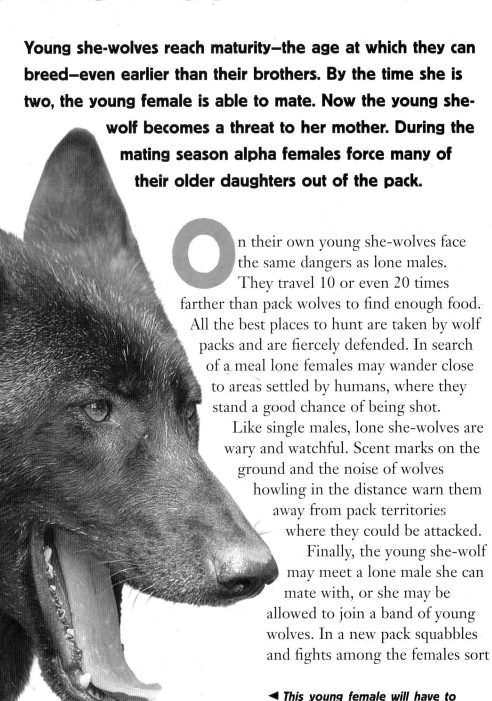

On their own young she-wolves face the same dangers as lone males. They travel 10 or even 20 times farther than pack wolves to find enough food. All the best places to hunt are taken by wolf packs and are fiercely defended. In search of a meal lone females may wander close to areas settled by humans, where they stand a good chance of being shot.

Like single males, lone she-wolves are wary and watchful. Scent marks on the ground and the noise of wolves howling in the distance warn them away from pack territories where they could be attacked. Finally, the young she-wolf may meet a lone male she can mate with, or she may be allowed to join a band of young wolves. In a new pack squabbles and fights among the females sort

◄ *This young female will have to reach the top rank in her pack before she is allowed to breed.*

► *The female usually digs her den in well-drained soil near a supply of drinking water.*

out which animal is the strongest. The most powerful she-wolf becomes the new alpha female—the only wolf in the group to become pregnant, give birth, and raise cubs.

Shortly before her cubs are born, the alpha male or the other females may help her dig a long underground burrow. As her birth pains begin, the female takes to the den. If she has a large litter of eight cubs or more, it may take up to six hours for all the babies to be born.

▼ *Giving birth to a large litter may take a long time. At least the female has the comfort of her own den.*

Ranking among females

Female wolves in the pack follow a strict ranking order, established by fighting. Like the alpha male, the top female leads the group and protects the younger wolves. She may decide when and where the pack goes hunting and mark the borders of the territory with her scent. The other females help rear her cubs.

Body parts

Gray wolves are the largest wild dogs. An adult male wolf may measure up to seven feet (2.1m) long from nose to tail-tip and weigh as much as 75 pounds (35kg). Female wolves are slightly smaller than the males and weigh about 11 pounds (5kg) less.

Like most members of the dog family, wolves have five toes on their front feet and four toes on their hind feet. They run on their toes, which means that they take long strides. Their long, strong legs make them tireless runners. Wolves can lope along for many hours if necessary. They can also sprint at

Sense of smell

A wolf's sense of smell is many times more powerful than a person's. The animal can identify thousands of different smells. Even young cubs can pick up very faint scents of distant creatures. The wolf's keen hearing also helps it hunt its prey.

◄ *With its ears pricked forward this wolf is listening for its next meal.*

▲ *Wolves have to be able to run fast and for long distances even on snow.*

up to 28 mph (45kph) for a short distance to catch swift prey.

Wolves have long snouts, narrow chests, and lean, slim bodies. Their whole shape is slender and smooth, which makes them fast over the ground. The thick fur all over their bodies keeps them warm and dry even when the weather is cold and wet.

Jaws and teeth

▼ *Four long, sharp canine teeth give a wolf a fearsome appearance.*

Wolves have very strong jaws that can bite down with great force. In the front of its mouth the wolf has four long, pointed teeth called canines. They are the main weapons used to seize its prey. At the back of the mouth are large, jagged teeth called carnassials. As the wolf's jaws close, they work like scissors, shearing meat into bite-size chunks.

The dog family

Wolves and other wild dogs are all members of a larger group of animals called carnivores. Cats, bears, raccoons, hyenas, and seals are all types of carnivores. All these animals feed mainly on meat.

The family of carnivores began to evolve (develop) a very long time ago. Scientists know about their development from fossil remains that have been found, including ancient bones and teeth.

About 40 to 50 million years ago a family of animals called the *Miacoidea* lived on Earth. They were about the same size and shape as modern mongooses and lived in trees. Very gradually, over millions of years, the miacids came down from the trees and became swift-running hunters on prehistoric grasslands. Modern dogs and wolves slowly evolved from these early creatures.

There are over 30 species (kinds) of modern canids—members of the dog family. Jackals, dingoes, and foxes are all canids that are quite closely related to wolves. Wild dogs are found on every continent except

▼ *The Simien wolf (also known as the Simien jackal) is found in only a few places on high mountains in Ethiopia, Africa.*

Coyotes

Coyotes are found in North and Central America. About half the size of wolves, they have long, slender noses, large pricked ears, and long legs. Unlike wolves, coyotes are not usually found in packs.

Antarctica. Dingoes, the wild dogs of Australia, did not develop there but arrived with early humans more than 4,000 years ago.

All members of the dog family have keen senses of smell and hearing. They feed mainly on meat and hunt live prey that they grip with their sharp canine teeth. Most have long legs, and all are strong runners. All have long snouts and furry coats, and most have long, bushy tails.

▶ **The black-backed jackal is found on grassland and in dry woodland across East and southern Africa.**

▼ **The dingo was probably brought to Australia from Southeast Asia by humans.**

Dire wolves

Dire wolves were prehistoric wolves that lived in North America about two million years ago. They are now extinct, but we know of their existence from remains found in ancient tar pits in California. Dire wolves were giant predators, half as big again as modern wolves. During the last Ice Age these ferocious creatures hunted prey as large as woolly mammoths.

Where wolves live

Wolves live only in the northern hemisphere, the northern half of our planet. They once roamed across North America, Europe, and most of Asia, and were the world's most widespread predator. However, people have feared and hunted wolves for centuries, and today they are much rarer. There are few wolves left in western Europe, India, and in most of the United States.

Through the centuries wolves have been driven out of many areas as the land was taken over and used by people. In many places open grasslands were plowed up to make cropfields or fenced off to keep grazing animals such as sheep and cattle. Elsewhere forests were cut down for wood or to make space for towns and pastures. As more and more land was taken, wolves retreated to remote parts of the far north.

Wolves are still common in Alaska and northern Canada, and across the Atlantic in Siberia, in northern Russia, and in other parts of Asia where there are few people. Across the northern hemisphere wolves live in many different habitats (types of country), from frozen wastes to snowy mountains, dark pine forests, leafy woodlands, rolling grasslands, and even deserts. Wolves that live in different areas have slightly different habits.

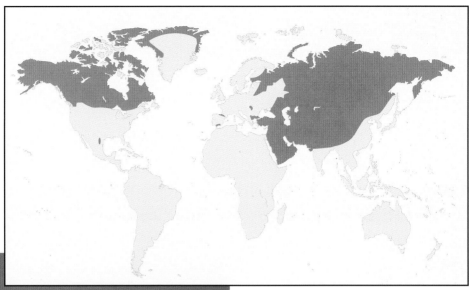

► *Places in the world where wolves are found.*

▲ *In the far north wolves have almost white fur so they blend in with the snowy surroundings of the Arctic.*

◄ *Wolves are perfectly at home in forests.*

For example, they hunt different prey, depending on what animals are found there.

The size of wolf territories also varies from region to region. In the far north, where prey is scarce, wolves have huge territories because they need a large area to hunt in. In places where food is plentiful, territories are often much smaller.

Indian wolves

Wolves were once common throughout India. However, large numbers have been hunted and killed in the last 200 years, and now they survive only in smaller, scattered areas. Some live in remote forests, but others are found close to towns. They slink in under cover of darkness to steal scraps from garbage dumps.

Different types of wolves

Scientists who study wolves have identified about 30 different subspecies (types) of gray wolf in different parts of the world. They are often named for the places where they live, for example, Mexican and European wolves. Two of the main subspecies are timber wolves, which live in the forests of North America, and Arctic or tundra wolves, which live in the far north.

Wolves from different areas vary in size. Some are large, and others much smaller. The thickness of their fur varies too. Wolves that live in very cold places have thicker fur than wolves that live in warmer regions. These adaptations (changes) help the wolves survive in the areas where they live. Scientists think the size of different types of wolves is related to the size of their prey. Arctic wolves are the largest. They hunt muskoxen and caribou—some of the biggest prey.

The color of wolves' fur also varies from region to region. Some wolves have white or very pale fur. Others are tawny, gray, or black. Different types of wolves are often colored so that they blend with their surroundings. This camouflage (natural disguise) makes it easier for them to sneak up on their prey.

Wolves that live in deserts are often small and sand-colored. Their pale coats reflect the sun's rays, helping them keep cool and disguising them. Wolves that live in forests are medium-sized and often gray. The timber wolf of North America is an example.

▼ *Only very small numbers of Mexican wolves survive in the wild.*

◀ Many areas where European wolves were once found have now been built on or farmed. This wolf is luckier than most: It receives protection in a Polish reserve.

▼ An Arctic or tundra wolf sharpening its teeth on a caribou antler.

Arctic wolves

Arctic or tundra wolves live in the snowy wastes of the far north. Their very thick coats help them keep warm in howling winds and freezing weather. All wolves shed their fur at certain times of year. They have a thick winter coat and a thin summer one. Arctic wolves' coats also change color with the seasons. In summer many of these wolves have dark fur. In winter many are pure white, so they can hide against the snow.

Wolves and people

In early times Native Americans admired wolves for their strength and cleverness. Many warriors and chiefs were named after wolves. Healers called on the spirit of the wolf to give sick people strength.

In medieval Europe things were very different. Before guns were invented, wolves were bolder and less scared of humans. They would slink into lonely settlements to steal sheep, goats, and cattle. Many people believed they also preyed on humans, particularly children.

Towns and villages hired special huntsmen to track and kill wolves with the help of large dogs. Later, the invention of guns made hunting easier. When white settlers arrived in North America, the same thing happened. Tens of thousands of wolves were shot, trapped, or poisoned. Wolves were also killed for sport and for their warm fur.

Wolves had been wiped out in much of Europe by the 1800s and by the 1950s in the United States. However, in the last 50

▲ *In places where wolves are protected, they begin to lose their fear of humans. This Arctic wolf is approaching a park guard at Ellesmere National Park, in Canada.*

years people's attitudes toward wolves have been changing. People realize we no longer need to fear wolves. Like Native Americans, many people now appreciate the courage, skill, and loyalty of the wolf.

Today, wolves are making a comeback in some areas where they had died out. Wolves bred in captivity have been released in national parks. Local farmers are paid money if wolves kill their stock. Many people now understand the wolf is part of a natural world that is fast disappearing—and that we have a duty to protect.

► **Wolf skins for sale in a Norwegian market.**

▼ **Wolves are still hunted in many parts of the world. This one has been shot in a Polish forest.**

Domestic dogs

From toy poodles to giant St. Bernards, all breeds of domestic dogs are thought to be descended from the wolf. "Man's best friend" has been around for at least 12,000 years. By Roman times many breeds of dog had already appeared. Wolves and their close relatives, coyotes, dogs, and dingoes, can all still interbreed to produce hybrids such as coy-wolves and wolf-dogs. These semiwild dogs are very difficult to tame.

29

Further reading

Dog
by Juliet Clutton-Brock
(Knopf, 1991).

Endangered Wolves
by Casey Horton
(Benchmark Books,
1996).

**Foxes, Wolves, and
Wild Dogs of the World**
by David Alderton
(Sterling Books, 1998).

In Praise of Wolves
by R. D. Lawrence
(Holt, 1986).

**My Little Book of
Timber Wolves**
by Hope Marston
(NorthWord Press, 1997).

Out Among the Wolves
by John Murray (Alaska
Northwest Books, 1993).

Trail of the Wolf
by R. D. Lawrence
(Rodale Press, 1993).

The Wolf
by Jeremy Bradshaw
(Boxtree, 1991).

Wolves
by R. D. Lawrence
(Sierra Club Books,
1990).

Wolves
by Susan Ohanian
(SRA, 1994).

Wolves
by Seymour Simon
(HarperCollins, 1993).

**Wolves and Their
Relatives**
by Erik Stoops and
Dagmar Fertl
(Sterling Books, 1997).

Web sites
www.californiawolfcenter.org
www.wolf.org
www.wolfcenter.org
www.wolfpark.org
www.wolftracker.com

Useful addresses
**Conservation Society for
Wolves and Whales**
27013 Pacific Highway S,
167, Kent, WA 98032.

Friends of the Wolf
P.O. Box 21032, Glebe
Postal Outlet, Ottawa,
Ontario, Canada K1S 5N1.

**International
Wolf Center**
1396 Highway 169, Ely,
MN 55731.

Mexican Wolf Coalition
207 San Pedro NE,
Alburquerque, NM 87108.

**North American
Wolf Foundation**
Wolf Hollow, Ipswich,
MA 01938.

Glossary

alpha female and male: the most senior pair of animals in a wolf pack. The alpha pair are usually the only wolves to breed.

camouflage: the colors and patterns on animals' bodies that blend with their surroundings and so help them hide from enemies or from prey.

canid: a member of the dog family. Wolves, coyotes, jackals, dingoes, and domestic dogs are all types of canids.

canines: the sharp, pointed teeth at the front sides of the wolf's mouth, which it uses to bite its prey.

carnivore: an animal that eats mainly meat.

cub: the young of animals such as wolves.

den: a burrow used by animals such as wolves to protect their young.

evolve: when an animal species changes very slowly so that the animals are better suited to the conditions in which they live.

habitat: a type of area where certain animals live, such as a forest or a desert.

hierarchy: a social order among a group of animals.

litter: a group of animals with the same mother, born at one time.

pack: the name given to a group of wolves.

predator: an animal that hunts other animals for food.

prey: an animal that is hunted for food.

regurgitate: when an animal coughs up food, often to feed its young.

territory: an area that an animal uses for feeding or for rearing its young, and that it defends against others of its kind. Many different animals use territories.

Index